慶祝

Celebrating

Gwenyth Swain

Chinese translation by David Tsai

small world

Milet

For my grandfather Alfred P. Coman,
who knew how to celebrate the small things in life

To find out more about the pictures in this book, turn to page 22.
To find out more about sharing this book with children, turn to page 24.

The photographs in this book are reproduced through the courtesy of: © Trip/J. Sweeney, front cover; © Trip/G. Pritchard, back cover; Ling Yu, p. 1; Portland Rose Festival Association, Photo: Gayle Hoffman, p. 3; John S. Foster, p. 4; © Jeffrey J. Foxx, p. 5; Russell L. Ciochon, p. 6; © Trip/M. Jelliffe, p. 7; © John Elk III, p. 8; Ruthi Soudack, p. 9; Jeff Greenburg, pp. 10, 16; © Trip/B. Gibbs, p. 11; Lyn Hancock, p. 12; © Brian A. Vikander, p. 13; IPS, p. 14; © Trip/S. Grant, p. 15; © Elaine Little/World Photo Images, p. 17; Nancy Smedstad/IPS, p. 18; © Stephen Graham Photography, p. 19; © Trip/M. Ockenden, p. 20; Voscar, The Maine Photographer, p. 21.

Celebrating / Small World Series

Milet Publishing Ltd
6 North End Parade
London W14 0SJ
England
Email info@milet.com
Website www.milet.com

Second dual language edition, 2004
First English–Chinese dual language edition published by Milet Limited in 2000
All dual language editions published by arrangement with Carolrhoda Books, Inc., a division of Lerner Publishing Group, U.S.A.

Copyright © Carolrhoda Books, Inc., 1999

ISBN 1 84059 132 3

Printed in China

當你做了很棒的事時，你會慶祝嗎？
Do you celebrate
when you do something great?

你可以為冬天而慶祝。

You can celebrate winter.

你可以為春天而慶祝。
You can celebrate spring.

慶祝一趟公園遊，

Celebrate a trip to the park

或是國王的來訪。
or a visit from the king.

當有特別的事情時，
去換個新髮型。
When something special happens,
get a new hairdo.

穿上你最好的衣裳。

做一些你從來沒有想過要做的事！

Put on your best outfit. Do something
you never thought you'd do!

當遊行隊伍經過城裡時，
跑去坐在別人的肩上。
Get on someone's shoulders
when a parade goes through town.

或加入遊行隊伍，四處搖旗。

Or join the marchers
and wave a flag around.

如果那天好像有點特別，
就拿個鼓敲敲打打，
When the day seems special,
bang a drum

或跳跳舞。
or dance a dance.

賽賽跑。

Run a race.

碰碰運氣。

Take a chance.

人們慶祝許許多多的事，
不管是新或舊；是老或少。
People celebrate many things,
old and new.

你也有一些想要慶祝的事嗎？
Is there something
you want to celebrate, too?

想一想你和家人共處的時刻
Think of time you spend with family

或你與朋友共度的時光。
or days you spend with friends.

慶祝每一天和節日。
Celebrate holidays and every day.

無論何時何地都可以慶祝！
Celebrate no matter where,
no matter when!

More about the Pictures

Front cover: In North Korea, children celebrate the fiftieth anniversary of the Workers' Party.

Back cover: This girl is dressed up for the Notting Hill Carnival, which takes place in a West Indian neighbourhood in London, England.

Page 1: People in Taiwan celebrate with a parade.

Page 3: This girl in Portland, Oregon, celebrates winning a ribbon in a local parade.

Page 4: Winter snows make kids in Ruby, Alaska, smile.

Page 5: This boy in Georgia, a country in southeastern Europe, celebrates the coming of spring.

Page 6: It's time for fun at a park in Hanoi, Vietnam.

Page 7: An Ashanti chief visits during a festival in Ghana, a West African country.

Page 8: A girl in Mali, in West Africa, wears a new hairdo for a special day.

Page 9: For the Holi festival in India, people pour bright-coloured powder on their heads and celebrate the end of winter.

Page 10: You have to be tall to see what's going on in Saint Petersburg, Russia.

 **Page 11:** On a London street, English children wave their flag, the Union Jack.

 **Page 12:** In Nunavut, a territory in northern Canada, a young Inuit child learns to play the drum.

 **Page 13:** A girl in Laos, a country in Southeast Asia, dances a traditional dance to wish people well.

 **Page 14:** In Côte d'Ivoire, a country on the west coast of Africa, a young man takes part in a race.

 Page 15: To celebrate Thanksgiving, these American children dress up a little differently—as the Statue of Liberty.

 **Page 16:** In Latvia, in northern Europe, an older woman and her friends celebrate the birth of a lamb.

 **Page 17:** Going to school is a good reason to celebrate for these children in Tokyo, Japan.

 **Page 18:** In Minneapolis, Minnesota, a grandmother and grandchild celebrate their Ukrainian heritage.

 **Page 19:** Three friends enjoy just being together in Omaha, Nebraska.

 **Page 20:** Celebrating Halloween is popular with these children in London, England.

 **Page 21:** A young girl celebrates summer in Quebec City, Canada.

A Note to Adults on Sharing This Book

Help your child become a lifelong reader. Read this book together, taking turns as you both read out loud. Look over the photographs and choose your favourites. Sound out new words and come back to them later for review. Then try these "extensions"—activities that extend the experience of reading and build discussion and problem-solving skills.

Talk about Celebrating

All around the world, you can find people celebrating. Discuss with your child the things people celebrate in different countries. What holidays, birthdays, and other events do you celebrate? How do your celebrations differ from celebrations in other parts of the world? How are they the same?

Plan Your Next Celebration

With your child, plan your next holiday, birthday, or other celebration. Ask your child what decorations will be needed. Make a list of foods you will need. Talk about inviting friends and family. Then work together to complete your plans and make this celebration special.